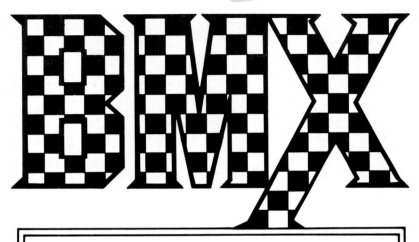

A PHOTO-FACT BOOK

BY
S. TROPEA

KIDSBOOKS, INC.
7004 N. California Ave.
Chicago, Illinois 60645

Printed in the U.S.A.

The Story of BMX

The BMX rider is a new breed of cyclist and BMX is a new kind of riding. Beginning around 1969, the sport emerged from the daredevil excitement of cross-country motorcycle riding, or motocross. Kids riding "Stingray" bikes—low, small-wheeled versions of the traditional bicycle—began to duplicate the jumps, turns and spins of motocross. Called "dirt-bike racing" at first, the sport had no rules, no special equipment, no professional riders and no organization. What it did have was lots of eager fans.

The first riders "popped wheelies," went airborne off home-made ramps and raced one another over trails through local parks or vacant lots. Some, particularly those in California, rode their bikes over motocross tracks after the motorcyclists had gone home. For others, riding a factory Schwinn with a banana seat and coaster brakes off curbs or through parking lots was as close to cross-country riding as they would get.

Soon, factory bikes and sidewalks weren't enough to satisfy the growing interest of young riders in high-performance biking. They built neighborhood dirt tracks with real ramps and jumps. They modified their bikes, stripping off kick-stands, chain-guards, reflectors and all other extra weight to gain speed. And with the increased performance of their bikes, they developed new and daring riding techniques. The day of the simple wheelie was over. The sport began to get serious.

Refinement was the next step. A motocross promoter in California, Ernie Alexander, saw the possibilities. He built a real track modeled on the hair-raising jumps, tight turns, waterholes and banked sections of a motocross track. Soon the word spread and racers came from miles away.

Bicycle manufacturers noticed the new trend in bikes. The larger companies chose to wait and see where the new sport was going. But small companies didn't. They built special bikes with custom frames, heavy duty tubing and handlebars, and brakes to match. The BMX bike was born.

If the first serious riders were in California, kids in other states weren't far behind. Homemade tracks and trails and pro-style motocross tracks dotted the country, but you had to be a rider to know where they were. BMX wasn't in the news and it wasn't organized. There were no well-known riders, no factory teams and no race sponsors, just enthusiastic kids who were learning to ride special bikes like nobody had ever done before. It all changed in 1976.

Ernie Alexander knew the sport needed a champion. He promoted seven national races hoping to find one. Scot Breithaupt entered all of them and emerged as the Grand National Champion. Within a year, professional BMX racing was in the headlines—not only in its own paper, *The Bicycle Motocross News* (where the name BMX came from), but in daily newspapers as well.

The American Bicycle Association (ABA) and National Bicycle Association (NBL) were formed. Prizes for the Number One Pro rider climbed from $20 for a first prize to $13,000. Factory teams representing bike builders and equipment manufacturers sponsored riders. Free-style, or trick-riding, went from wheelies to the midair magic of tabletops. And in bike shops from coast to coast, kids looking for a bike and a challenge headed for the high-tech BMX, the favorite set of wheels of a new generation.

Bikes

The "Stingray" style bike was the original dirt-track bike. Low to the ground on 20″ wheels, it was really a small version of a regular balloon-tired bike, and a far cry from the lean, mean machines called BMX. The stingrays and similar bikes were built by well-known bicycle manufacturers such as Schwinn, Ross and others. Names like Mongoose, Red Line, Diamond Back, Torker and Hutch were answers to bikers' needs for specialty machines. Riders needed strength, low weight, maneuverability, power and speed in their bikes to handle the demands of motocross riding and, later, free-style. The new

builders gave them exactly what they wanted, and more.

The three main components of a BMX bike are 1. the frame, 2. the drive train and braking and 3. the wheels and steering. Each has many separate parts and each fills a specific need.

The frame is the "body" of the bike. It is made of welded tubular steel. The best bikes use chrome-moly or chrome-alloy steel which is strong and lightweight. The joints are welded and reinforced by extra pieces of metal for additional strength. Frames may be painted or chrome-plated. The fork is a part of the frame and serves two functions, support and steering. Together the frame and fork are called the frameset.

A bike moves by converting the up and down pedaling motion of its rider's legs to circular motion through a sprocket (chainwheel). The sprocket drives a chain that turns the rear wheel. In a BMX bike the drive train must be strong and responsive.

Stopping a bike is as important as making it go. The brakes, either hand-operated caliper type or reverse pedal coaster type, do the job. Racing bikes use caliper brakes, while free-style bikes call for coaster brakes.

BMX wheels and tires are quite different from the spidery wheels of a 10-speed. They are 20″ in diameter with heavy-duty tires. Racing wheels are spoked to save weight, but free-style bikes may have plastic or nylon mag wheels to stand up against the extra stress of trick riding. Mag wheels are one-piece with spokes and rim molded together. Spoked wheels have metal rims, usually made of lightweight aluminum. The treads for each use are also different. Racers need ground-gripping knobbies for traction. Free-stylers need smoother treads for precise control.

Steering is accomplished by turning the front fork with handlebars. The fork swivels within the head tube to turn the wheel.

BMX bikes are factory-built or custom-made. Factory-built bikes are standardized machines. Every chrome Hutch Pro Star, for example, is identical. A custom bike is built to the buyer's requirements. Different parts from different companies are used to create a one-of-a-kind machine.

While a BMX bike may look simple, it is a complex and

sophisticated machine of many critical parts. Most riders, whether recreational or pro, eventually add their own touches to their bikes to personalize them and to increase performance.

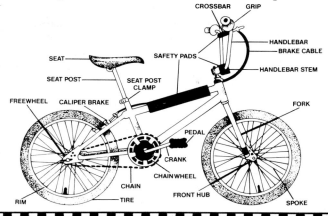

The Heart of a BMX Bike

Frameset—Consists of two separate parts, the frame and the fork. Made of strong, lightweight, tubular chrome-moly or chrome-alloy steel. The bike is built around the frameset.

Handlebar and stem—A "Y" or steerhorn-shaped bar with a crossbar for extra strength joined to the fork by a short shaft, the stem. The bike's steering and control center.

Crank—The bike's geared "engine" that converts pedaling to rotary motion. Supports the pedals and front chainwheel. Can be one-piece steel (stronger, less expensive) or three-piece aluminum (lighter weight).

Wheels—Mag wheels are strong, one-piece plastic or nylon composition with built-in spokes and hub, especially suited for free-style, but too heavy for racing. Lightweight aluminum rims called "alloys" with 36–48 spokes are most common.

Hubs—The wheel's "axle." The hub bolts to the front or rear dropouts (deep notches in the frameset) so the bike can roll.

Sealed hubs require less maintenance and last longer than loose-ball hubs, which are more precise and preferred by serious riders and pros.

Tires—Can have knobby treads for maximum traction in mud and sand, or tight, smoother treads for street and hard-surface riding. Usually black or black with narrow white sidewalls, but also come in colors.

Freewheel—A wheel with a hub that engages for forward pedaling but not for back-pedaling (braking). Caliper brakes are required.

Brakes—Two types, caliper (hand-operated) and coaster (foot-operated). Caliper brakes squeeze rubber pads on jaw-like calipers against the front and rear wheel rims. Coaster brakes slow and lock the rear wheel hub only.

Pedals—Rat-trap pedals have jagged teeth for good foot to pedal traction. Platform pedals use studs to keep the foot from slipping off.

Saddle—The seat, raised high on the seat post to help stabilize the bike, is rarely used for sitting when underway. The lightweight "shotgun" saddle is aerodynamically designed and is preferred for racing.

Grips—The handles at the ends of the handlebars. Round, soft rubber grips are more comfortable and easier to hang onto than hard plastic grips that can be slippery and cause blisters.

Standing pegs—Short, sturdy, built-in pegs that let the rider stand on various parts of the frame for free-style tricks.

Number plate—Required for racing. A light plastic frame that attaches to the handlebar to display rider's number.

Buying a BMX Bike

A BMX bike is to an ordinary bicycle what a Jeep is to the family car. It is a specialty machine designed for high performance, durability and reliability. A BMX bike is not just for riding. It's for *using!* Above all, it is highly personal, reflecting the rider's distinctive needs and ability.

Buying a BMX bike is not something to take lightly, especially by serious riders. First-time buyers should pay as much attention to what they need as to what they want. The following guidelines can simplify choosing the BMX bike that's right.

Determine Need—Will the bike be for racing, free-style or both? Racing bikes are lighter weight than free-style bikes. Pure free-style bikes are unsuited for racing. Recreational bikes can do both, but lose the high performance of the specialty bikes.

Judge Riding Skill—Is the rider a beginner, intermediate or expert? A new rider needs a sturdy bike for learning the basics rather than a high-tech machine for high performance. As skill develops, the rider can move up.

Select Correct Size—All BMX bikes have 20″ wheels, but combining different framesets, handlebars, seats and other components lets them fit small, medium and large riders.

Test Ride First—The rider should try out different bikes and different sizes before buying. The ideal way to learn the feel and fit of a bike is to test ride bikes belonging to friends.

Get Outside Opinion—Friends, other riders and bike shops are excellent sources of information. Magazines and books provide technical advice and expert opinion.

Shop Around—BMX bikes cost from $150 to $500. Customized bikes can cost even more. The best bike for a rider isn't always the most expensive.

Equipment and Accessories

The high performance of a BMX bike requires equally high levels of safety. The rules and regulations of sanctioned races and free-style events are specific about the use of helmets and other safety requirements. The recreational rider should keep in mind that safe riding is fun riding. Proper equipment can make the difference between a thrill and a serious injury.

Except for helmets and mouth guards, the BMX rider can substitute standard items such as sturdy jeans, shirts and gloves for those products made especially for the sport.

Helmets—High impact plastic with inside padding to assure a proper fit is essential. Full face helmets offer the best face protection. Open face helmets require a mouth guard.

Goggles and Visors—Goggles should fit the face and the helmet for complete eye protection. Visors shield the eyes from glare.

Pants—Made of durable nylon with stretch panels, "leathers" (named after their original material) have built-in knee pads, shin-guards and reinforcement. Measure carefully for fit.

Jerseys—Thicker material provides more protection in a spill while lightweight, vented jerseys are cooler. Some have built-in elbow pads.

Gloves—Gloves are optional, but protect the hands from injury and blisters.

Elbow Guards—Provide extra protection, especially for free-style riders.

Rad Pads—Cushioned pads for the top tube and handlebar crosstube.

BMX Riding

BMX riding is not ordinary bicycle riding. It's a specialty. Racing and free-style call for a variety of techniques. In racing, the idea is to keep the bike on the ground and under control. Getting air wastes time. In free-style, it's control of the bike in the air that's important. The basics are easy to learn. Practice makes them perfect.

Jumping—Choose an open dirt space that is free of rocks and other obstacles. Build a 5–6″ high, hard-packed dirt mound midway down the practice run to allow room for starting and stopping.

Begin with slow rides over the mound without leaving the ground. Gradually build up speed until the bike leaves the ground. To control the take-off and landing, stand over the center of the bike in a moderate crouch with the feet and pedals parallel to the ground, using the legs and arms to keep the bike upright and to absorb shock.

Land on the rear wheel first by pulling back lightly on the handlebars on take-off. Pulling too hard flips the bike backward. Lean forward to correct a flip. Bend the knees slightly.

Cornering—A racing rather than a free-style technique, controlled cornering increases speed around the course and prevents wipe-outs. Sliding wastes time and energy.

Knowing when a bike is going out of control is a matter of feel. To get the feel, practice brake slides. Enter a turn and hit the brakes. When the bike begins to slide, lean into the turn, bracing with the inside leg. Start slowly before building up to higher speeds.

Once the feel of sliding is familiar, practice taking fast left- and right-hand corners. Keep the weight forward and the inside foot down as a brace while leaning into the corner. Remember to try to avoid slides during a race.

Cross Ups—Cross ups are basic free-style stunts. To do a "kick-out," twist the hips after the bike leaves the jump to force the rear end to one side. A "tabletop" is a maximum-

effort kick-out that puts the bike parallel to the ground. In a "one-footer," take one foot off the pedal and put it back on before the bike lands.

Competition

Early competitors raced or performed free-style stunts among themselves. There were no sanctioned (approved) or sponsored events. As the BMX became popular, regulating organizations were formed, standards were adopted and companies began to financially support events and individual riders. Major racing and free-style competitions with big prizes are now common coast to coast.

Racing

BMX racing is divided into separate heats called motos. Racers are grouped by age and ability so that those in a single moto are evenly matched. A moto sheet posted before the meet lists which riders are in each moto with equal numbers of up to eight riders in each.

Riders in each moto race three times. Prizes are awarded to the top riders who may also go on to compete in the main event if one is scheduled. If there are many riders, semi-mains (one race elimination heats) are held to determine main-event riders. Scoring is by the low-point system or the transfer system. In low-point scoring, the winner gets one point, second place two points and so on. Those with the lowest scores ride in the main event. The transfer system automatically puts the winner of each moto into the semi-main or main event. The ABA uses the transfer system. All other BMX organizations use the low-point system.

A BMX race or moto lasts only about 40 seconds. Speed is king. But speed without control on a BMX course is not possible. The hills, twists, turns and jumps require a high degree of skill or the rider will crash at worst or lose precious seconds at best.

The BMX course is a specially built, one-way, twisting,

obstacle-filled dirt track. The starting gate is at the top of an 8–10 foot-high-hill. Between the start and finish lines are a number of mounds, banks and curves. Negotiating the course in a tight pack of riders demands concentration, endurance and tactics. Each rider develops a style based on these fundamental techniques.

Starts—Keep both feet on the pedals and the bike balanced against the starting gate. Hold the head up and the back straight. The moment the gate drops, throw the weight forward while pulling up sharply on the handlebars and thrusting down on the forward pedal.

Jumps—Keep as low to the ground as possible when jumping. Getting too much air costs time and energy and risks losing control. To speed jump, do a wheelie just before hitting the jump, then quickly push the front wheel down as the bike clears the jump. Keep the weight to the rear to avoid going over the handlebars on landing.

Passing—Strong riders can command a moto with pure speed and energy. To equalize a strong rider, execute passing techniques in the turns. Prepare before entering, then ride through smoothly, without sliding, with the inside foot balancing the bike. In a *block pass* the rider takes the inside line, goes into the turn low and exits high. This blocks other riders at the same time. The *slingshot pass* is the opposite of the block pass. Here the rider enters the turn high (on the outside) and comes out low.

Tips—Warm up by riding 15–20 minutes before the race. If possible, check out the track beforehand. Most importantly practice, practice, practice.

Free-Style

Free-style or trick BMX riding requires good balance, steady nerves and a good imagination. Basic tricks such as wheelies and stationary balancing are well known. The imaginative rider is the one who puts them together in new and daring ways with safety always first.

Tricks are performed on flat surfaces, banked surfaces or in quarter and half pipe ramps. Unlike racing, a trick rider can practice or perform almost anywhere and any time, even inside if the weather is bad.

Start with basic bike handling and jumping. Practice jumping until you've got it down perfectly. Now you're ready to try cross ups. It's important not to move to the next step until the first trick is perfected. Combine simple tricks into a routine, then work in more complex moves. Remember to think each trick through before trying it.

Glossary

Alloys—Spoked aluminum wheels.

BMX—Short for *bicycle motocross,* BMX refers to track racing, stunt riding and the specialty bikes used in the sport.

Berm—A banked curve on a BMX motocross track, there are a minimum of three on every track.

Block pass—A passing move. Stay next to bike to be passed, go in low and come out high.

Bunny hop—A jumping technique for getting over obstacles.

Crank—To pedal hard, e.g., "He's really cranking."

Daytona turn—A high-banked turn on a track, with the steepest part in the last half of the turn.

Flatland—Flat surface free-style without using ramps.

Free-style—Trick or stunt riding, but not racing.

Freewheel—A hub that allows the crank to be pedaled in reverse.

Getting air—When the bike leaves the ground. Too much air costs time and energy in a race. In free-style, more air means more time and space to perform an airborne stunt.

Gnarly—Difficult or hard to do.

Hang time—The time the bike and rider are in the air.

High flying—To get mega-air.

Holeshot—The first rider out of the gate, the first rider to reach an obstacle or the first rider to reach the first turn.

Kamikaze—A rider or stunt at the maximum edge of controlled performance.

Knobbies—Tires with heavy treads (knobs) for maximum dirt-grabbing traction.

Moto—An individual motocross race or heat.

Quarter pipe—A severely curved (a quarter of a circle) free-style ramp. Also, *half pipe* (a half-circle ramp).

Rad—Short for radical. Wild, far-out and fearless. Pushing skill and machine to the max.

Rad pads—Pads on the bike to prevent or reduce injury to the rider.

Serious—Describes a difficult maneuver or a skilled performance.

Slingshot pass—A passing move. Go in high and outside, come out low.

Speedjump—The preferred way to take a jump to avoid getting too much air. Wheelie on entering the jump, shift the weight to the rear and keep pedaling.

Tabletop—The maximum kick-out stunt. The rider kicks his bike parallel to the ground after getting air and then lands upright. In racing, a flat-topped obstacle on a track.

Ultra-rad—Rad to the max.

Wheelie—Riding on the rear wheel, with the front wheel off the ground. Used in racing to set up a speedjump.

Wired—A maneuver or technique that is perfected or in control, as in, "He's got that stunt wired."

Whoop de doo—Three or four successive humps on a track.

Photographs by Focus on Sports.